P9-EDT-125

Mendelssohn

THE GREAT COMPOSERS

MENDELSSOHN

by
MICHAEL HURD

THOMAS Y. CROWELL COMPANY
New York

First published in the United States of America in 1971

Printed in Great Britain

L.C. Card 75-121384
ISBN 0-690-53105-2
0-690-53106-0 (Lib. Ed.)

1604595

Contents

Illustrations

9

Music Examples

Acknowledgements

In writing this book my chief sources of information have been the Mendelssohn biographical studies by Eric Werner (Macmillan, 1963) and Philip Radcliffe (Dent, 1954), and the pioneer work of Sir George Grove, as it appears in the first edition of *Grove's Dictionary of Music and Musicians*. Though it is no longer possible to distinguish the exact degree to which I am indebted to these works, or indeed to recall the many casual sources of information that have come my way during a lifetime's interest in the subject, I am delighted to have an opportunity to record my thanks.

The score of the E flat Quartet and the letter to William Batholemew on the subject of *Elijah* form part of the British Museum's Mendelssohn collection and are here reproduced by kind permission. Portraits of the composer and his family are here reproduced by kind permission of the British Museum (Print Room) and the Radio Times Hulton Picture Library. All efforts to trace the present whereabouts of the manuscript of the *Elijah* aria, once owned by J. Curwen & Sons Ltd., have failed, and it is here reproduced from Stephen Stratton's *Mendelssohn* by kind permission of J. M. Dent. The extracts from Mendelssohn's works appear in simplified arrangements of my own devising.

Sincere apologies are offered to any person or body whose contribution to this book has been overlooked.

Mendelssohn

I

The Mendelssohn Family

Jacob Ludwig Felix, the second of Abraham and Lea Mendelssohn's four children, was born in Hamburg on 2nd February 1809. Whatever personal reasons the family may have had for calling him only by his last name, their decision now seems singularly appropriate. Few composers have been born to greater good-fortune, or in more felicitous circumstances. The Mendelssohns were not only intelligent and cultured, they were also rich.

It had not always been so. Felix's grandfather, Moses the 'son of Mendel', came from a very different world. His father was a humble schoolmaster who earned scarcely enough to feed his wife and children; and Moses himself was born hunchbacked and ugly. But he was also born with a genius for philosophy and an iron will. He was determined to win through to a better kind of life. And so, in 1743, at the age of fourteen, he left his native Dessau and set out for Berlin.

He walked every inch of the way. When he arrived, footsore and weary, before the great city walls, he made his way round them until he came to the Rosenthaler Gate—the only gate through which Jews like himself might enter. It is said that when the guard came to record the day's events, he wrote:

> Today there passed through the Rosenthaler Gate, six oxen, seven pigs, one Jew.

Whether the incident is true or false hardly matters: the facts of Jewish life were harsh enough. In the eyes of German law, Jews enjoyed few rights —indeed, laws were passed especially to humiliate them. They were subject to every kind of insult; and when popular feeling ran high, even their lives were in danger.

Germany was not alone in its barbarous treatment of the Jews. The whole of Europe regarded them with the utmost suspicion. For they were held together not by allegiance to a king or country, but by their religious faith. Wherever they went they took their faith with them, and so, instead of accepting local beliefs and customs, remained stubbornly Jewish—thus creating a State within a State. Moreover, their religious beliefs were, in several important respects, at variance with those of the Christian Church.

Jews thus became the natural enemy: the ever-present, but wholly imaginary threat to European society. At different times and in different places these fears gave rise to petty and vexatious laws. Jews were obliged to pay special taxes. They were allowed to buy food only at particular times of day. They could not enter certain professions, nor study at the universities. They were forced to live only in one part of the city—the ghetto. And sometimes mere harassment gave way to wholesale terrorism and slaughter.

Against this background of violence and prejudice, the young Moses Mendelssohn contrived, somehow, to prosper. He learned new languages: French, English, Latin, and Greek. He read deeply in mathematics, philosophy, and European literature. He rose from abject poverty, to become first a tutor, then a book-keeper, and then a partner in a silk manufacturing firm. At the same time, he won a reputation as an outstanding philosopher. His books were read throughout Europe, and brought him the friendship and admiration of many famous men. And because he was also very brave, he used his influence to speak out for Jews everywhere, in the name of justice and humanity.

Despite his awkward physical appearance, Moses Mendelssohn married happily and in due course became the father of six children. His second son, Abraham, was born in 1776, and it was he who was to become the father of the composer. Sandwiched between two famous men, Abraham was quick to appreciate the irony of his situation. Brushing aside his own considerable gifts, he would say: 'Formerly I was known as the son of my father. Now I am known as the father of my son!'

In 1797, at the age of twenty-one, Abraham Mendelssohn obtained a junior appointment in the Paris banking house of Fould & Co. He worked hard, and by 1803 had risen to become the bank's chief cashier. In the following year he resigned and, in partnership with his brother Joseph, set up a banking and import firm of his own in Hamburg. His marriage to Lea Salomon, in December 1804, further improved his fortunes. She was the daughter of the Prussian court jeweller, and the grand-daughter of the great banker Daniel Itzig.

By nineteenth-century standards, Lea Mendelssohn was a highly educated woman (she even read Homer in Greek—though, we are told, she kept this accomplishment a secret, lest she be thought 'unfeminine'). She was a good pianist, and studied for some time with Johann Philipp Kirnberger, who had been a pupil of Bach. Though not beautiful, she was generally considered 'attractive' and graceful. She was, in short, a very desirable match for an aspiring young banker.

Mendelssohn's
birthplace
in Hamburg

The young couple suited each other well and seem to have been extremely happy. Lea: charming, intelligent, and witty; something of a snob, perhaps, when it came to social ambitions; was nevertheless an excellent mother. Abraham: stern and efficient; governed in all his actions by the belief that the gifted man had a duty to strive after perfection and so, by his example, help others; was also loved and respected. Together they combined attitudes upon which an affectionate and wholly united family could be built.

It is important to underline the strength of the Mendelssohn family bonds, for they came to exert a remarkable influence over the way in which Felix's career and personality were to develop. All important decisions were family decisions. Nothing was done without consultation. Living on sufferance even in the land of their birth (as all Jews had to in those days), only the family could be relied upon at all times and in all weathers.

After their marriage, Abraham and Lea settled in Hamburg. They lived in a large, comfortable house known as Marten's Mill, and it was there that three of the four children were born. In 1811, however, shortly after the birth of Rebecca, when Fanny was six and Felix two, they were forced to disguise themselves, flee from Hamburg and take refuge in Berlin.

The reasons for the upheaval are complex. When Napoleon defeated Prussia in 1806, he forbade all trade with England, with whom he was still at war. Hamburg lived by its shipping and therefore depended entirely upon such trade. Merchants were faced with a simple alternative: either they could obey Napoleon and see themselves ruined, or they could become high-class smugglers and make a fortune. They soon saw where their duty and their profit lay.

For some years an illicit trade with England went on merrily. It was just a matter of knowing how to bribe the French officials. But then Napoleon suddenly clamped down: he sent Marshal Davout to deal with the situation. Opinions are now divided as to whether the Marshal actually expelled the blockade-breaking merchants, or merely arranged matters so as to control the smuggling for his own benefit. At all events, certain families thought it wiser to leave in a hurry. Among them were the Mendelssohns.

Since, from the Prussian point of view, their activities had been entirely correct and patriotic, the Mendelssohns had no difficulty in re-establishing themselves in Berlin. When fighting broke out again, in 1813, they supplied money to buy equipment for the troops and helped to set up an army hospital. Jews they might be, but no one could doubt their patriotism. Abraham Mendelssohn was so highly thought of by his fellow citizens that they elected him to the Berlin Municipal Council.

Thus, with financial success and public honour achieved, the Mendelssohn family had one remaining problem to consider. Should they continue to be faithful to the Jewish religion, or should they allow themselves to be converted to the Protestant Church?

Lea Mendelssohn seems to have been almost eager to make the change.

She was probably influenced by her brother's example: he turned Protestant, and at the same time dropped the tell-tale surname with which he had been born and became instead the irreproachable Mr. Jacob Bartholdy.

Abraham Mendelssohn was less willing to change his religion, but recognized that if he did so he might help his children. At first he went half-way: he had the children baptized and brought up as Protestants. It was only some time later that he and his wife felt ready to join them. And then, as an outward symbol of the change, he also agreed to add the name Bartholdy to his own—just as his father had coined a new surname when he began to climb out of the squalor and misery of his humble beginnings.

II

Childhood

There could be no doubt that the Mendelssohn children were musical. The two youngest, Rebecca and Paul, learned to sing and play instruments. Fanny, the eldest, became a fine pianist and even tried her hand at composition. But it was Felix who was the exception: his talent amounted to genius.

Much as they loved music, neither of the Mendelssohn parents wanted it to take a special place in their children's education. They encouraged music as they encouraged all the arts; but it was a solid general education that came first. The idea that one of the children should become a professional musician simply never entered their heads.

The routine laid down for their general education was, by modern standards, frighteningly severe. They got up at five in the morning and began lessons immediately after breakfast. They did not, however, go to school. Instead they had private tutors who could supervise every minute of the day. Idleness was unknown. When they wanted to relax, they read serious books, took lessons in drawing and painting, went for long, strenuous rides on horseback—and, of course, practised hard at their music.

Far from resenting severe discipline, the children seemed to thrive on it. Yet they were not docile or cowed. They simply followed family tradition and used their energies seriously. They were exceptional children, living in an exceptional family.

Both Felix and Fanny studied the piano. First with their mother, and then, when it was obvious that they had real talent, with Ludwig Berger. Felix also took violin lessons with Carl Hennings, attended the Berlin Singakademie to have his voice trained, and studied harmony and counterpoint with Karl Friedrich Zelter.

Of all his tutors, Zelter made the greatest impression on Felix. He was an excellent craftsman and an inspired teacher. He was also something of a personality and numbered among his friends such important figures as the philosopher Hegel, the dramatist Schiller, and, above all, the renowned Goethe.

Zelter knew exactly how to stimulate the interest of a sensitive, highly imaginative boy. He set him teasing riddles that made the study of counterpoint seem more like a game. He was fully aware that his pupil had the same kind of youthful genius as the young Mozart, and treated him accordingly.

At nine years old, Felix had already proved the unusual quality of his talents by appearing on the concert platform as a pianist. And then he began to compose—not just one or two isolated pieces, but a great stream of works of all shapes and sizes. In the year 1820 alone, he seems to have written more than fifty pieces: trios, sonatas, songs, partsongs, cantatas. The following year's work was equally impressive: five sinfonias for string quartet, nine fugues, a great many songs and motets, and two one-act operas: *The Two Pedagogues* and *Soldiers' Love*.

Even though his parents were reluctant to admit that their eldest son was a musical prodigy, they could not ignore the sheer industry and enthusiasm. His interest in music was, it seemed, a serious matter, to be weighed with caution. In the meantime they did nothing to discourage him.

As it happened, opportunities for home music-making were everything a young composer could desire. The family house on the New Promenade was pleasant and spacious. There were rooms large enough for concerts on a grand scale, and it became the family custom to give elaborate musical parties every other Sunday. Few important musicians passed through Berlin without attending, and so, for Felix, it meant a unique extension of an already thorough musical education.

He was not just a listener, however. He conducted the orchestra—even, it is said, when he was so small that he had to stand on a footstool to be seen by the players. He played the violin and the piano: sometimes alone, sometimes with Fanny, while Rebecca sang and Paul played the 'cello. But most important of all: he composed music for the concerts.

The chance of hearing a work almost as soon as you have written it is something that few young composers have enjoyed. The value of the experience is beyond description—it is the perfect way of learning to be a composer. With Zelter there to criticize, the boy could scarcely fail to develop rapidly.

The Sunday concerts were only one feature of musical life in the Mendelssohn home. With four talented children and a host of distinguished visitors, impromptu recitals were likely to spring up at any time. And sometimes admiration for a particularly famous visitor would in itself prompt further activity. There can be no doubt that the string of one-act operas that Felix began to compose after 1821 was a direct result of meeting Carl Maria von Weber when he was in Berlin for the triumphant performance of *Der Freischütz*.

It was Zelter, however, who brought about the most important meeting of Mendelssohn's young life. Towards the end of 1821 he took him to Weimar to visit his friend Goethe, who was universally regarded as the great genius of the age.

The prospect of such a meeting threw the entire family into a state of great excitement and apprehension. Goethe held himself notoriously aloof from all but the most respected musicians, and it was clear that he was prepared to acknowledge a twelve-year-old boy only because Zelter had spoken so warmly of his talents. The visit to 'His Excellency' must be regarded as an a exceptional honour. Moreover, Felix was leaving home for the first time. His father warned him to 'sit properly and behave nicely, especially at table; speak clearly and sensibly, and try as much as possible to keep to the point of the conversation'. His sister Fanny insisted that he keep his eyes and ears wide open, and threatened that 'if you cannot repeat every word that falls from his lips, I will have nothing more to do with you'. His younger brother and sister danced about in delighted envy, while his mother wept a little, and then made sure that he had everything he might need on so momentous a journey.

She also found time to write to her sister-in-law, to boast, just a little:

> Imagine, the little scamp is to have the good luck of going to Weimar with Zelter for a short time. He wants to show him to Goethe! You will understand what it costs me to part from the dear child, even for a few weeks. But I consider it such an advantage for him to be introduced to Goethe, to live under his roof and receive his blessing. I am also glad of this little trip as a change for him; for his impulsiveness sometimes makes him work harder than he ought to at his age.

Early in November the 'little scamp' kept his promise and sent back the first of the many letters that descri e the visit:

> Now listen, all of you. Today is Tuesday. On Sunday the Sun of Weimar—Goethe—appeared. In the morning we went to church, where they gave us half of Handel's 100th Psalm. The organ is large, but weak—the Marien-Kirche organ, small as it is, is much more powerful. This one has fifty stops! Afterwards I went to the Elephant inn, where I

sketched the house of Lucas Cranach. Two hours later Professor Zelter called and said: 'Goethe is here—the old gentleman has arrived.' In a flash we were down the steps and in Goethe's house. He was in the garden and just coming round a hedge. Isn't it strange, dear Father, that was exactly how you first met him! He is very friendly, but I don't think any of the pictures are like him.

The visit lasted sixteen days. Goethe was seventy-two and was not at first inclined to take a twelve-year-old musician very seriously. With mock severity he began to test the boy's abilities, setting him improvisations and Bach fugues, exactly as if he had been an examination candidate. Soon however, his manner changed. He produced precious manuscripts for the boy to play from—first Mozart, and then Beethoven.

And so the visit continued, and with each day Goethe's affectionate interest in Felix Mendelssohn grew, until Felix, at the end, was able to write to his parents:

. . . I play here much more than I do at home: rarely less than four hours, and sometimes six or even eight hours. Every afternoon Goethe opens the Streicher piano and says: 'I haven't heard you at all today—now make a little noise for me.' Then he sits down beside me, and when I have finished (I usually improvise) I ask for a kiss or take one. You cannot imagine how good and kind he is to me. . . .

And because Felix Mendelssohn was still, after all, a child, Goethe wrote a parting verse for him, as an accompaniment to some fanciful silhouettes that had been cut for his amusement:

> *If witches' broomsticks thus can bound*
> *Over the solemn score,*
> *Ride on! through wider fields of sound,*
> *Delight us more and more,*
> *As you have done with might and main,*
> *And soon return to us again.*

Felix took him at his word. He was to visit Weimar many times, for he knew that Goethe was now his friend.

Back in Berlin the routine of intensive general education and industrious home music-making continued. He appeared for the second time on the public concert platform in March 1822, and again at the end of the year. At the same time he continued to write music: six more sinfonias for string

The opening of the first movement of Mendelssohn's Quartet in E flat written at the age of eleven

orchestra, five concertos for various instruments, two piano quartets, a number of piano sonatas and vocal pieces, and a full-scale opera called *The Uncle from Boston*. All this was accomplished in a year which saw the entire family absorbed in an elaborate tour of Switzerland, which lasted from June until September.

The family tour was no casual affair. It was carried out in great style: the six members of the family, four close relatives, tutors for the children, and servants for everyone. And like all such expeditions at this period it was undertaken in a spirit of further education—people simply did not go 'on holiday' in the modern sense.

Even the outward journey was planned with at least half an eye to improving Felix's experience of music. Armed with a letter of introduction from Zelter they stopped off at Cassel and called on the famous composer Louis Spohr. He looked with approval at the boy's music, and soon they were on the best of terms. A similar break at Frankfurt led to a lifelong friendship with Ferdinand Hiller, who was two years younger than Felix and almost as talented.

Switzerland itself delighted everybody. The children took out their sketchbooks and, in much the same spirit as the modern traveller takes photographs, began recording all the views. To Felix, however, sketching was more than just a pleasant pastime. He took it seriously and developed a very considerable talent, far above the usual amateur daubing. Like his music, his drawings are neat and economical—fine lines and delicate shading, and a strong sense of form.

He also found time to write long letters to his friends in Berlin, explaining in great detail the new and fascinating things he had heard and seen. Zelter, for example, was treated to a delighted account of Swiss yodelling —complete with musical examples taken down on the spot. 'This kind of singing,' he observed, 'sounds harsh and unpleasant when it is heard near by, or in a room. But in the valleys, the mountains, or the woods, when you hear it mingling with the answering echoes, it sounds beautiful. . . .'

His trained academic ear was affronted, however, by what he heard in the Bernese Oberland. Here the girls were accustomed to sing in parallel fifths, thus breaking one of the most sacred rules of polite music. Felix hastened to explain their crime to Zelter—perhaps with a sly grin at the thought of the many times when his own grammar had taken a tumble.

On the return journey Felix remembered his promise to Goethe and the whole family stopped off at Weimar. Had there been any doubt about the old poet's delight in the company of his young friend it was now dispelled for ever. Felix, he said, was like the young David, come to cheer Saul with his music.

At last they arrived back in Berlin and Felix busied himself putting the finishing touches to his latest opera *The Uncle from Boston*. Soon it was ready for performance. A small stage was rigged up in the largest of the family's drawing-rooms and rehearsals began. After the first performance Zelter stood up before the entire audience and, turning to his fifteen-year-old pupil, said:

> My dear boy, from this day you are no longer an apprentice, but a full member of the brotherhood of musicians. I proclaim you independent, in the name of Mozart, Haydn, and old father Bach.

III

Success and Failure

Not everyone was quite as convinced of Felix's genius as Zelter appeared to be. Jacob Bartholdy, for example, was far from happy, and, as Felix's uncle, he felt obliged to make his views known. A musician's career, he said, was no career for a gentleman. Who could be sure that this youthful brilliance would not fade as the lad grew to maturity? What would happen to him then? His disapproval communicated itself to Abraham Mendelssohn, who immediately fell victim to the most dreadful forebodings.

Fortunately Felix had friends to speak for him, and gradually the family began to take notice. In the end, Abraham Mendelssohn decided to consult the most important musician he knew: Luigi Cherubini. If he thought that Felix had the makings of a first-rate composer (nothing less would do for a Mendelssohn) then he would be allowed to make music his career. If not, he would have to turn his mind to something else. Confident that all would be well, Felix agreed to his father's plan and together they set out for Paris.

Far from being overawed by the serious nature of the trip, Felix was highly critical of everything he saw and heard. He met all the great musicians of the day—Auber, Meyerbeer, Rossini, Liszt—but he was not impressed. He reported back to his sister, and even she was a little shocked by his youthful arrogance. 'Liszt,' he wrote, 'plays very well: he has many fingers, but few brains . . .'; 'Meyerbeer gave a lecture on the nature of the French Horn. . . . I laughed so much I nearly fell off the chair . . .'; 'Rossini, the great Maestro Windbag . . .'; 'Auber . . . a grey-haired old man, a pupil of Cherubini and the darling of the public, ought at least to be able to orchestrate, especially in our times, when the publication of Haydn, Mozart, and Beethoven scores has made it so easy!'

He was not even alarmed at the prospect of meeting the legendary Cherubini, for he had already decided that he was 'an extinct volcano, still throwing out occasional sparks and flashes, but quite buried in ashes and stones'. And although Cherubini had the reputation of being bad-tempered and difficult to please, Felix was not the least bit surprised to see him raise his eyes from the Piano Quartet he had brought as a sample of his work and say: 'The boy is talented. He will do well. He has already done well.'

Cherubini's verdict was enough to set Abraham Mendelssohn's fears at rest. And having once decided to let his son become a professional musician, he let him go his own way. Unlike Mozart's father, he did not try to direct his son's career. He was always willing to give advice and, as we shall see, would sometimes make it plain that he thought his son had taken a wrong turning, but he did not interfere.

There was thus no need for Felix to stage any kind of revolt against parental control. He slipped from under it, without fuss or bother, and enjoyed perfect freedom. Or was it, after all, only the illusion of freedom? There remains the lurking suspicion that the very fact of not having to fight left him, to a large extent, dependent on his father's judgement. Everything hinges on the way in which you interpret his career and general development—for some critics stoutly maintain that his music never changed: that it reached its highest point when he was sixteen and seventeen and there remained, never to improve or deepen.

But just how remarkable that early maturity was, soon became evident. By the end of 1825 he had more than fulfilled Cherubini's declaration of confidence. In that year he completed his Octet for strings.

The Octet is, without doubt, the most astonishing achievement of any youthful composer. Not even Mozart or Schubert wrote with quite such brilliance and assurance at this age. The music is not just precocious, it is mature and deeply satisfying; and the work remains, even to this day, one of the masterpieces of chamber music.

Not everyone, however, can accept the Octet as chamber music pure and simple. Much of the writing is orchestral in style—exciting tremolos, broad unison themes that sweep through the instruments in a very full-blooded manner. Mendelssohn seems to have been aware of this, for, in a preface to the original score, he wrote:

This octet must be played by all instruments in symphonic orchestral style. *Pianos* and *fortes* must be strictly observed and more strongly emphasized than is usual in pieces of this character.

Perhaps it would be wiser to regard the Octet as the last and greatest of the miniature symphonies he wrote for the family's private string orchestra.

Success and Failure

The most original of the four movements is the third—the scherzo. According to Fanny, who followed all her brother's work with the keenest interest and was at this time his most valued critic and greatest source of encouragement, the movement is an attempt to capture the atmosphere of a witches' meeting on Walpurgis Night. Goethe had included just such a scene in *Faust*, and it was this that set Felix's imagination alight.

To most people the idea of witches gathering on the Brocken during the night before May Day is rather frightening. The belief was certainly enough to unnerve villagers all over Europe, who for centuries performed ceremonies on May Day itself that were designed to undo the mischief of the previous night. But Mendelssohn's witches do not sound at all harmful. Their music is light and fantastic and magical, but never frightening.

This fairy-like delicacy is uniquely Mendelssohn's. Only one other composer (Berlioz, in the 'Queen Mab' scherzo from *Romeo and Juliet*) ever surpassed it. But Mendelssohn returned time and time again to the same atmosphere, so that it became one of the finger-prints of his style.

The Octet was an enormous success. Mendelssohn himself made a popular piano-duet version, and later orchestrated the scherzo for concert performance. The score was not published until after his death, however. For he was inclined always to cling to his music, rewriting passages again and again, until he was satisfied that nothing more could be done to improve them. Fluent and effortless though his music may appear, perfection was not achieved without a struggle.

Within a year, Mendelssohn had proved that the Octet was no mere passing flash of brilliance. He added another masterpiece to the world's concert repertoire: the Overture *A Midsummer Night's Dream*.

Shakespeare's play had always been a great favourite with the Mendelssohn family, and Felix had made it especially his own. Now he produced music fit to be mentioned in the same breath. Again it was the idea of spirits light as air that stirred his imagination. The opening woodwind chords leave no doubt that the curtain has risen on a moonlit, magic scene:

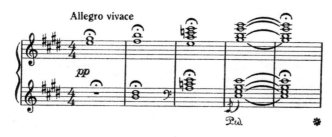

31

and the fluttering violins that follow can only be the beating of delicate fairy wings:

But Mendelssohn's overture also makes room for the comedy of Shakespeare's play. The rustics, Nick Bottom, Peter Quince, Francis Flute, Robin Starveling, Tom Snout, and Snug the joiner (who appears to have no Christian name), are conjured up with equal skill. Even the plaintive 'Hee-haw' of Bottom, translated into an ass, is faithfully recorded:

And it is important to remember this side of Mendelssohn's genius. Had he wished, he might have been a great master of the comic.

A Midsummer Night's Dream: Nocturne

32

Moses Mendelssohn (1729–86), celebrated philosopher and grandfather of Felix Mendelssohn

Mendelssohn's parents,
Abraham and Lea,
drawings by Wilhelm
Hensel

For all the sunny charm of his youthful works, it would be a great mis-
take to think that everything in Mendelssohn's life was equally sunny and
charming. One incident, in 1824, may serve to illustrate the uneasy position
the family occupied in German society, and the kind of tensions this uncertainty could produce in a sensitive young artist. The family had gone to
Dobberan, a popular seaside resort on the Baltic, for a short holiday. There,
walking one day in the street, Felix and Fanny were set upon by a gang of
hooligans who shouted 'Jews!' and spat and threw stones. Felix defended
his sister and brought her safely back to their lodgings. But the incident
upset him, and, shortly afterwards, he broke down in a flood of tears and
bitter protests.

This was not the first time he had endured insults because of his religious
background. In 1819 a young German prince had stopped him in the Berlin
streets, to spit at his feet and shout, 'Hep, hep, Jew-boy!' And something of
the kind was to happen in later years, as we shall see, when he offered himself as a candidate for the directorship of the Berlin Singakademie. On the
whole he was able to conceal this darker side of his life. But the insults left
their mark and made him increasingly sensitive to criticism of any kind.

So far as music was concerned, he had yet to face real criticism and disapproval. True, his family and his teachers had always been ready to speak
their minds—but only in the way of friendliness and out of a genuine desire

Success and Failure

to help. In his artistic life, Felix Mendelssohn had been sheltered from the harsher realities.

The first revelation came in 1827 with the performance of his full-length opera *The Wedding of Camacho* at the Berlin Royal Opera House. Like most operas, *The Wedding of Camacho* reached performance only after a long string of petty intrigues had been defeated. The manager of the theatre, Count Brühl, was willing to give the work a chance. But Gasparo Spontini, the music director, set his mind against it. Spontini was famous as the composer of grand spectacular operas—such as *La Vestale* (in which the heroine is saved from death by a thunderbolt) and *Olympia* (which introduced a live elephant on to the stage). Comic opera meant nothing to such a man. Moreover, he was very suspicious of Mendelssohn, whom he regarded as too young, too rich, and too great an admirer of his particular enemy, Weber. He criticized the opera relentlessly and then, as if to pour scorn on the whole project, agreed to a performance.

Although the opera house was full of family friends and well-wishers, the new work was not a success. Applause after the first act was enthusiastic. After the second act it was noticeably lukewarm. Before the curtain fell on the last act, Mendelssohn had fled the theatre and could not be persuaded to return. His fears were all too fully confirmed by a hostile criticism that appeared next day in the influential *Schnellpost*. And when the leading tenor fell ill, he seized the opportunity to let the opera disappear from the boards once and for all.

Such experiences are commonplace in the uncertain world of opera. Most composers would have been angry and hurt, but would then have shrugged and gone on to write more operas and press for revivals of those that had failed. But Mendelssohn allowed himself to be completely discouraged. Not only did he begin to harbour an increasing dislike for Berlin, but he also began to behave oddly towards the whole idea of writing an opera. He declared, loudly and at every opportunity, that this was his one ambition; but when it came to choosing a libretto, he was equally enthusiastic in finding excuses for turning it down. Apart from a short, but delightful operetta, *Son and Stranger*, written in 1827 to celebrate his parents' silver wedding anniversary and performed privately within the family circle, he made only one serious attempt to write an opera. But this work, *Loreley*, grew to little more than a handful of sketches and was left unfinished at his death.

IV

Mendelssohn and Bach

In 1825 the Mendelssohn family moved from their large house on the New Promenade to an even larger one on the Leipzigerstrasse. At first their friends were surprised. The Leipzigerstrasse was on the very outskirts of Berlin, and to live there was almost like being exiled in the country. But when they saw the house, they began to understand. It was magnificent: a small palace, standing in spacious, park-like grounds, enchanting in every way.

For Abraham Mendelssohn the new house represented the very pinnacle of social and financial success. It was a vindication of everything his father had suffered in the long struggle from obscurity. In the face of such solid evidence, there could be no doubting that the Mendelssohns had arrived.

Leipzigerstrasse 3 became the centre for a brilliant intellectual circle. The Sunday concerts, of course, went on as before. But the house was also a meeting place for poets, philosophers, and scientists. If you had not yet been welcomed by the hospitable Mendelssohns, then you could hardly consider yourself part of the highest Berlin intellectual society.

Felix, still little more than a boy, found it all very exciting. It was exactly the stimulus his precocious brilliance needed. He was able to sharpen his wits on some of the greatest minds in Europe. And although he diligently attended lectures at the University of Berlin, from 1825 until he matriculated two years later, he might just as profitably have stayed at home—for home was a university in itself.

There were, however, dangers. His mother pressed him to write the kind of brilliantly effective piano music that would make an immediate impression on her guests. But he was interested in writing music that had to be listened to with the utmost attention—the austere, contrapuntal motet *Tu es Petrus*, for example, which he wrote as a birthday present for Fanny; or the A minor String Quartet, which reflects his interest in Beethoven's last quartets (then regarded by most people as totally incomprehensible). Con-

35

fronted with works of this seriousness, his mother began to lament that 'nothing fresh, enjoyable, or lively comes forth any more'.

It is greatly to his credit that he felt able to withstand her loving tyranny and go his own way, stretching his talents by continually facing new challenges.

His chief ally was his sister Fanny. It was to her that he confided all his musical dreams, and her advice that he treasured beyond even that of professional musicians. The bond between brother and sister had always been deep. As they grew older it became, if anything, deeper.

Yet even here there were dangers to be guarded against, and Felix was well aware of them. As he grew older and more independent, his sister began to pry into his affairs. Remonstrations led to outbursts of anger and jealousy, followed by equally painful scenes of remorse. It was not until her marriage to the painter Wilhelm Hensel that Fanny felt able to relax her vigilance over her beloved brother. Only then did her intense and over-possessive love turn to a mature affection of lasting value to them both.

The position that Fanny Mendelssohn occupied in her brother's life and thoughts should not, however, be underestimated. Though his own marriage was to prove as happy as hers, it was, as we shall see, her cruelly sudden death that hastened his own. Within six months he too was dead.

But this is to anticipate events by twenty years. In 1827 Mendelssohn's concern was not with thoughts of death, but with plans for a resurrection. He had made up his mind to perform Bach's *St. Matthew Passion*.

Even before his death in 1750, Johann Sebastian Bach was generally considered to be first a great organist, second a learned pedant, and third a rather old-fashioned composer. Few of his works had been printed. Anyone wishing to study them had to rely upon manuscript copies, which could only be obtained with great difficulty.

At the beginning of the nineteenth century interest in Bach began to increase. In 1802 Forkel's great biography appeared, and thereafter a few brave London publishers started to print some of the keyboard music. More important, perhaps, was the living chain of interest that was still in existence: musicians who had been taught by Bach's own pupils. One such musician was Carl Zelter. He had been a pupil of Johann Kirnberger, who had studied with Bach from 1739 to 1741.

When Zelter became conductor of the Berlin Singakademie he included in their concerts some of Bach's motets. As a child, Mendelssohn had been brought up on Bach's *Preludes and Fugues*, and now the experience of hearing the motets fanned his interest into a blaze of enthusiasm. When he learned that Zelter actually possessed a manuscript copy of the legendary *St. Matthew Passion* he was beside himself with curiosity. He expressed himself so forcefully and so frequently on the subject that his grandmother arranged for another copy to be made. She gave it to him for Christmas.

Something of the awe in which Bach was then held can be gathered from comments made by the singer Eduard Devrient when Mendelssohn began to try out parts of the Passion during private concerts at home. 'Felix,' he wrote, 'had so profoundly studied the score—almost identifying himself with it—that he mastered all its problems with ease. Thus what had previously been considered a secret language now became natural and familiar to us.'

Mendelssohn, eagerly backed up by Devrient, was desperately anxious to give the *St. Matthew Passion* some kind of public performance. He decided to approach Zelter for the loan of the Singakademie choir.

At first Zelter refused to have anything to do with the scheme. He loved Bach's music, but he thought the *St. Matthew Passion* too difficult to perform —and certainly beyond the scope of a couple of 'snotty-nosed brats'. At this, Felix nearly gave up. But Devrient would have none of it. He ignored the old man's coarse expressions. He flattered and wheedled and at last squeezed a reluctant consent. The Singakademie would perform, and Felix would conduct.

Rehearsals began in February 1829. It soon became apparent that Felix knew exactly what he was doing. He had learned the work by heart and could correct his forces without glancing at the score. Zelter's fears subsided. At first he had hovered anxiously in the background, ready to leap to the rescue at the slightest sign of trouble. Now he simply relaxed and sat listening to the sublime music.

Word soon spread that Mendelssohn's venture was no mere exercise in musical archaeology. The *St. Matthew Passion* was, it seemed, a great and important work. Tickets were snapped up within twenty-four hours of being offered for sale, and hundreds of people had to go away disappointed. When the doors of the large concert hall were opened, on 11th March, every seat was occupied within ten minutes.

What followed was something that changed the musical world's attitude to Bach, once and for all. Exactly a hundred years after it had been written, the *St. Matthew Passion* came to life again, and from that moment Bach's music was saved for posterity.

But the triumph did not please every Berlin musician. To some it was simply further proof that a spoiled young amateur could do what he liked because he was rich and had influence. The murmurs grew. Spontini seized the opportunity to try to prevent a further performance of the *Passion*, arranged for 21st March, Bach's birthday. Fortunately he failed, but Mendelssohn undoubtedly suffered from his spiteful plots.

Worse was to follow. A difference of opinion arose between Mendelssohn and certain members of the Royal Orchestra, and they finally refused to play under his baton. Even the success of the *St. Matthew Passion* turned sour when it was whispered that the young Mendelssohn was really a musical scholar and not a creative musician at all.

Something had to be done, and quickly. Berlin began to stand for everything that was hateful and depressing. It was essential to get away, see fresh faces, enjoy new experiences.

Felix's mood coincided with his father's wishes for the final stages of his education. Like every wealthy young man of the period he was to make a Grand Tour of Europe, and in so doing 'improve himself and make friends'. The only question to be decided was the simple matter of direction. Which country did he wish to explore first?

There was only one answer so far as Felix was concerned. He would go to the country that the whole of nineteenth-century Europe stood in awe of. And so, on 18th April 1829, he said farewell to his family, boarded a boat in Hamburg and set sail—for England.

V

England

There were important reasons for making a break with his past way of life that perhaps even Mendelssohn did not fully appreciate at the time. He was twenty years old and already a mature, experienced composer. But each stage of his career had been watched over by his family. His father, generous and well-meaning, was a despot all the same. His mother, charming and sympathetic, was concerned with social snobberies and anxious for her son to shine always in the best possible light. His sister, intelligent and companionable, was alarmingly possessive. If he was to grow up and be himself, he had to get away.

In setting out for London, Mendelssohn was only doing what a great many continental masters had done before him and would continue to do, even to the present day. The London appetite for good music was insatiable. And London's readiness to pay for what it wanted was equally cheering. The road to professional success went, assuredly, through London.

To begin with, however, Mendelssohn had no intention of making a 'professional' visit. He was there to add further polish to his experience and education. He offered himself as a gentleman first, and as a musician some way after. It was only later that the musician in him gained the upper hand. Indeed, it is no exaggeration to say that it was because of his English visit that Mendelssohn came to accept himself as an artist and began, thereafter, to ignore the claims of social position.

Of course, he could not disguise the fact that he was a gentleman; polished, urbane, good-mannered and highly educated. And it was this that stood him in good stead with the English aristocracy and upper classes. It seemed to them astonishing that one so easy to accept on a social level could also be a superlative musician. Why, he was almost like one of themselves! He could dance and ride a horse. He was polite, he was witty, he could even speak English. He was handsome, elegant, stylish. Mendelssohn, it was plain, did not have to be classed as one of the servants.

39

England

When he arrived at the London Custom House on 21st April, however, his gentlemanly poise was far from certain. The crossing had been a nightmare. Half-way over, the ship's engines had broken down (how could you hope to rely on such new-fangled ideas?) and they had tossed about, helpless, until repairs had been done. The rest of the voyage was completed in the worst of weather. But there were friends to greet him, restore his shattered nerves, and bear him off in triumph to lodgings at 103 Great Portland Street. And then the social whirl began.

His friends, Carl Klingemann the diplomat and writer, and Ignaz Moscheles the pianist, had arranged everything: a visit to the Italian Opera at the King's Theatre in the Haymarket, where the great Maria Malibran was being paid phenomenal fees for singing in Rossini's *Otello*; a visit to Covent Garden, to hear Charles Kemble in *Hamlet*; a ball given by the Duke of Devonshire. He went everywhere and saw everything. English society regarded him as a 'distinguished foreigner' and treated him accordingly. The musical journal *Harmonicon* had already announced his arrival in the most reassuring terms:

> (He is the) son of a rich banker of Berlin, and, I believe, a grandson of the celebrated Jewish philosopher and elegant writer. He is one of the finest pianoforte players in Europe, and though a very young man, is supposed to be better acquainted with music than most professors of the art.

Felix Mendelssohn had every reason to be pleased with his first taste of London life.

As for London itself: it fascinated and bewildered him. It was so big, so noisy, so unpredictable. How could he explain it to a family accustomed to measure everything by the out-of-date standards of Berlin? And would they not be alarmed by the excited style of his letters?

> It is fearful! It is mad! I am quite giddy and confused. London is the grandest and most complicated monster on the face of the earth. How can I compress into one letter what I have experienced in the last three days! I hardly remember the chief events, and yet I dare not keep a diary, for then I should have to see less of life, and that I do not wish. On the contrary, I wish to take everything that offers itself. Things toss and whirl about me as if I were in a vortex, and I am whirled along with them. In the last six months in Berlin I have not seen so many contrasts and such variety as in these three days. Just turn to the right from my lodging, walk down Regent Street and see the wide, bright thoroughfare with its

arcades (alas! it is again enveloped in thick fog today) and the shops with signs as big as a man, and the stage-coaches piled high with people, and a row of vehicles left behind by the pedestrians because in one place the smart carriages have crowded the way! See how a horse rears up in front of a house because his rider has friends there; and how men are used for carrying advertisements extolling the achievements of performing cats; and the beggars and those fat John Bulls with their slender, beautiful daughters hanging on their arms. Ah, those daughters!

Mendelssohn made his first London appearance as a composer on 25th May at a concert given by the Philharmonic Society. At first it had looked as if the Society would not bother with his music. The president, Sir George Smart, had got it into his head that Mendelssohn 'made music only for fun', and that he 'did not need to do it at all', and that he was in England 'only as a gentleman and not as a musician'. It took some time to sort out the misunderstanding.

The success of the C minor Symphony at that first concert, however, dispelled any further doubts. The fashionable audience was delighted, and so were the newspapers. Mendelssohn thanked the Society for the excellence of their performance, and later asked if he might dedicate the symphony to them. They responded by making him an honorary member.

This was the first public honour he was to receive, and in many ways it was the most important. It came at a time when he badly needed reassurance. He never forgot that it was the universal English applause that 'lifted the stone from his heart'.

At the end of May he appeared as a solo pianist at a concert in the Argyll Rooms, astonishing his audience by playing Weber's difficult *Konzertstück in F minor* entirely from memory. In the middle of June the Philharmonic Society repeated the symphony that had been so much admired the month before, and on Midsummer Day they performed his new overture: *A Midsummer Night's Dream*. The audience was so delighted with this fresh proof of his genius that an immediate encore had to be given.

It was at this point that the work almost vanished from musical history. The composer Thomas Attwood was entrusted with the only score, but, in his excitement after the concert, he left it on the seat of a hackney carriage, which trotted away before anyone realized what had happened. Nor was he able to find it again. When Mendelssohn was told, he merely sighed and then sat down to write out the entire score from memory.

And so, after a final concert in mid-July, Mendelssohn found himself, at the age of twenty, an established favourite with English audiences. He had proved, beyond any doubt, that he was a composer of great originality, an uncommonly gifted pianist, and a first-rate conductor. He was young, he was handsome, he was a gentleman. What more could anyone ask of one man?

VI

Son and Stranger

With the London season at an end, Mendelssohn at last felt free to take a holiday. Travelling by stage-coach (fresh horses every ten miles, three stops a day for food, and one, perhaps, for the highwayman) he and Klingemann made their way north, through York and Durham, to Edinburgh.

From the civilized European point of view, Scotland at the beginning of the nineteenth century was a wild romantic place, full of mystery and the promise of adventure, its people strange, picturesque, almost barbarian. The novels of Sir Walter Scott, whose *Waverley* first came out in 1814, had placed it firmly on the map. It was the one country that every true Romantic longed to visit.

Like all good tourists, Mendelssohn and Klingemann were determined sightseers. They hunted for historic ruins and famous views. Mendelssohn made sketches, and Klingemann wrote verses to go with them—for there was much that would amaze and delight their friends at home. They took especial care to visit all the places associated with the ill-fated Mary Stuart— the ruined chapel where she had been crowned Queen of Scotland, the winding staircase down which her husband had dragged her shrieking lover to his death. It was even more romantic than they had dared hope: so much so, that Mendelssohn began to feel ideas for a 'Scottish' symphony stirring in the depths of his mind.

The music that he jotted down in Queen Mary's ruined chapel was to simmer quietly for twelve years before emerging as a full-fledged symphony. But a visit to the Hebrides brought a much quicker musical harvest.

They reached the island of Staffa on 7th August and made their way to the famous cavern of black basalt, moulded by some primeval volcanic change into awe-inspiring pillars. The islanders called it 'Fingal's Cave', after the great hero of Gaelic myth. Klingemann looked, but the sensible diplomat in him got the upper hand. He saw only something that reminded

43

him of a 'monstrous organ. Black, resounding, and utterly without purpose. . . .' Mendelssohn looked, and heard music.

'Fingal's Cave', Staffa

In order to make his parents understand the strange mood that had come over him in the cave, he sent them a copy of the twenty or so bars that had floated into his mind on the wind and waves. Out of them he was to make the finest concert-overture of its kind, and one of the landmarks of early romantic music: the overture *The Hebrides*.

Although it has been played thousands upon thousands of times since Mendelssohn finally shaped it to his satisfaction (in 1832), *The Hebrides* overture is as fresh and evocative as the first ideas that crept into his startled mind in August 1829. A high note on the violins conjures up an immediate picture of the broad, cloudless sky. A curling, wave-like theme in the lower strings and bassoon suggests the rolling sea below. Seldom have simpler means been used with greater effect. After Mendelssohn's overture, no composer, whether it was Wagner grappling with the tempestuous storms of *The Flying Dutchman* in 1841, or Smetana, thirty years later, contemplating

Son and Stranger

the quieter flow of the River Vltava, could write sea-music without borrowing from his example.

The Hebrides overture illustrates, very neatly, the ambiguous nature of all Mendelssohn's finest music. Its effect is 'romantic': it is superbly descriptive and poetic. Yet it is cast in a thoroughly 'classical' mould: a compact

Hebrides Overture

45

sonata form, as lucid and shapely as anything by Haydn or Mozart. This ability to hold a balance between classical form and romantic suggestion is something unique to Mendelssohn. No other nineteenth-century composer possessed the secret to quite the same degree.

Unfortunately, this refusal to countenance the extremes of nineteenth-century romantic passion has made Mendelssohn appear, to some critics, rather bloodless and lacking in feeling. But the passion is there. It is practised with restraint, and does not seek to overwhelm the listener with mere sensation. The idea of an outburst of wild emotion—the kind of thing he saw in Berlioz, whom he admired as a man, but detested as a musician—would have seemed to Mendelssohn no more than a sign of bad-breeding, to be avoided at all costs. It is arguable that in holding to this view Mendelssohn lost contact with the most powerful influence in nineteenth-century music, but he cannot be said to have been wrong. He was simply being true to himself and his background.

The Scottish tour continued, Mendelssohn recording his feelings sometimes in letters, sometimes in drawings, sometimes in music. At length it was time to make the return journey. They went by way of Liverpool, where Mendelssohn seized the opportunity of riding on the new Liverpool–

Manchester railway line. He was elated by the 'crazy speed' of the engine (it was all of 22 miles-an-hour) and it confirmed his view that England was the country of the future.

At Liverpool the two friends parted, Klingemann returning direct to London, and Felix travelling on alone into Wales in search of fresh delights. There he spent a pleasant interlude, at Coed-du, with John Taylor, a mining engineer, who had three pretty daughters. They observed him closely:

> Soon we began to find that a most accomplished mind had come among us, quick to observe, delicate to distinguish. There was a little shyness about him, great modesty. We knew little about his music, but the wonder of it grew upon us; and I remember one night when my two sisters and I went to our rooms how we began saying to each other, 'Surely this must be a man of genius. . . .'
>
> We observed how natural objects seemed to suggest music to him. There was in my sister Honora's garden, a pretty creeping plant, new at the time, covered with little trumpet-like flowers. He was struck with it, and played for her the music which (he said) the fairies might play on those trumpets. When he wrote out the piece (called a Capriccio in E minor) he drew a little branch of that flower all up the margin of the page. . . .
>
> Mr. Mendelssohn was not a bit sentimental, though he had so much sentiment. Nobody enjoyed fun more than he, and his laughing was the most joyous that could be. . . .
>
> He was so far from any sort of pretension, or from making a favour of giving his music to us, that one evening when the family from a neighbouring house came to dinner, and we had dancing afterwards, he took his turn in playing quadrilles and waltzes with the others. He was the first person who taught us gallopades. . . .

By the middle of September Mendelssohn was in London again, his head full of ideas for a new string quartet (Op. 12 in E flat). And at this point he would probably have returned to Berlin, for his sister Fanny was to be married in October. Unfortunately he was thrown from a carriage and injured his leg so badly that he had to retire to bed. Despite the bitter disappointment of missing the wedding, he allowed himself to be nursed back to health with as much patience as a man of his restless energy could muster. It was nearly December before he was able to set sail for home.

He returned with the score of a new operetta almost complete. It was more than a simple operetta, however: it was a present for his parents, to be performed in celebration of their silver wedding anniversary. He called it *Son and Stranger*.

And this, perhaps, was what he was. He had left Berlin unsure of himself, and uncertain of his standing as a professional musician. Now that he had proved that he could fend for himself, both as a man and as a musician, he was subtly changed. Even though he was not yet twenty-one, it was obvious to everyone that he had grown up.

Felix Mendelssohn aged about eleven

Fanny Hensel *née* Mendelssohn, Felix's sister, a drawing by Wilhelm Hensel

VII

European Travels

At the beginning of May 1830, Mendelssohn set out on the second stage of his Grand Tour. This time he headed south, travelling first with his father to Dessau (a pilgrimage to Moses Mendelssohn's birth-place?) and then continuing, alone, to Weimar, where Goethe was ready to welcome him.

Immediately the old friendship was resumed, and with it the old habits:

> In the morning he makes me play the compositions of the various great masters, in chronological order, for an hour, explaining to him in what respects they have advanced the art of music. . . .
>
> He did not want to hear anything of Beethoven's, but I said I could not let him off, and played the first movement of the C minor Symphony. It had an extraordinary effect on him. At first he said, 'This causes no emotion, only astonishment; it is grandiose.' He went on grumbling in this way, but after a long pause he began again: 'It is very grand, very wild; it makes one fear that the house will fall down. What must it be like when played by the whole orchestra!'

The fortnight in Weimar passed quickly and soon the time came for Mendelssohn to be on his way. From Weimar he went to Munich, then Salzburg, then Vienna—staying just long enough in each to form some idea of the state of music, make himself known to the leading musicians, and pay his respects to any friends or relations. Not everything he saw pleased him. Vienna, for example, far from being a shrine to the music of Haydn, Mozart, and Beethoven, seemed wholly given over to trivialities and was, in his eyes, 'a damned frivolous dump'.

Nor were conditions much better when he eventually reached Italy. True there were great paintings to examine, fine architecture and delightful landscapes to brood over; and, as the Grand Tour took him to Venice, Bologna, Florence, Rome, and Naples, he enjoyed all these things. But his

D   49

Scottish Symphony: third movement

letters home suggest a critical, wary eye, and a general feeling of not quite being able to approve of everything he saw. His industrious, earnest spirit could not accommodate itself to the leisurely ways of the south, and so he never fell in love with Italy in the way he did with England.

Throughout his wanderings, however, he was busy writing music. Like Mozart, he seems to have possessed enormous powers of concentration which made it as easy for him to compose in a jolting coach or an unfamiliar lodging as in the most private and comfortable study. During the Italian tour Mendelssohn was at work on *The Hebrides* overture; a setting of Goethe's poem *The First Walpurgis Night*, for chorus and orchestra; a symphony in D major (*The Reformation*); and the first stages of two more symphonies, the *Italian* and the *Scottish*. In between whiles he completed a number of choral works and piano pieces.

His method of composition seems always to have been the same: a sudden flood of ideas, followed by a comprehensive sketch of the entire work. Then there would come a long period of revision—often lasting for years, and sometimes preventing publication altogether. Three versions of *The Hebrides* overture exist. The *Scottish* symphony was not completed until 1842; and although the *Italian* symphony was said to be complete in 1833, he went on tinkering with it until the day of his death and never actually saw it in print.

Mendelssohn's obsessive search for perfection seems all the more astonishing in the light of the smooth, effortless quality that is one of the major features of his music. It flows like the spontaneous song of a bird. The doubts and difficulties he is known to have grappled with are wholly absorbed. The final product is serene and inevitable. But it is precisely this serenity that has led critics to dismiss his work as superficial. The truth is that few composers ever laboured more conscientiously to achieve their ideal of musical perfection.

Of all the romantic composers, Mendelssohn departs least from the classical idea of musical form. His symphonies and overtures may have poetic titles, but they depend for their ultimate effect on purely musical logic. *The Hebrides* overture takes its atmosphere from the sea, but, as we have seen, does not try to paint a picture of it in any detail.

The *Reformation* symphony makes use of two ideas, the Catholic 'Dresden Amen':

and the Lutheran hymn 'Ein' Feste Burg':

in order to suggest the opposing forces of the Reformation. But it does not try to tell a story. Nor do the *Italian* and *Scottish* symphonies. They borrow a little local colour (the dance rhythms of the Saltarello for Italy, the skirl of the bagpipe for Scotland), but only enough to give a picture-postcard impression of the country. The music may be tinged with poetry and romantic description, but it remains in all essentials a musical argument carried out in purely musical terms.

Mendelssohn's Italian tour took him as far south as Naples. He had wanted very much to go on to Sicily, but his father forbade it. Presumably it was thought to be too dangerous: if you did not fall victim to marauding bandits, you were sure to be engulfed by some volcanic eruption. At that distance from parental authority he might have disobeyed and said nothing; but he preferred to do as he had always done, only protesting that his ambition had been serious and ought not to be dismissed as a mere whim.

The leisurely return journey began in May 1831. Rome, Florence, Genoa and Milan; up into Switzerland, and across, through Augsburg, to Munich, where he arrived in September. Much of the Swiss part of the journey was made on foot, and included strenuous expeditions up mountains —of a kind that few ordinary travellers would care to undertake today. And all the while he made sketches, to include in his letters back home:

Italian Symphony: second movement

This is where I had my breakfast:

Weissenberg, *August 8th*

I sketched this on the spot with a pen, so do not laugh at my treatment of the water. I passed the night very uncomfortably at Boltigen. There was no room at the inn, owing to a fair, so I was obliged to lodge in an adjacent house, where there were swarms of vermin quite as bad as Italy, a creaking house clock, striking hoarsely every hour, and a baby that screeched the whole night. I really could not help for a time noticing the child's cries, for it screamed in every possible key. . . .

Munich was important for a concert he gave on 17th October. It included his C minor Symphony, the *Midsummer Night's Dream* overture, and the first performance of his new Piano Concerto in G minor, which he declared had been very hastily written in a matter of a few days. It is not perhaps one of most inspired works, but it is remarkably fluent and effective, and does suggest the immense professional skill he could now bring to a hurried, routine task.

When he left Munich he carried in his pocket a contract to write an opera for the Royal Theatre. Although, in the end, nothing was to come of the project, he was full of enthusiasm and declared that he would use Shakespeare's *The Tempest* as his subject. In deciding to have his libretto written in German he ran up against his father, who thought it would be best to have it written by a Frenchman and then translated (presumably because French Grand Opera was at that time highly successful). For once, he stuck to his point and won the day. But it is interesting to note that his father soon began to hint that it was time he gave up his dalliance with 'the spirits of air and water' and concentrated on more elevated subjects, and that the Shakespeare opera was quietly shelved.

From Munich, Mendelssohn moved on to Stuttgart, Frankfurt, Bonn and Düsseldorf, and then, in December 1831, to Paris. It was to be his last visit to the French capital.

Relaxing after the turmoils of the 1830 July Revolution, Paris was enjoying a period of great artistic activity. Honoré de Balzac, Alphonse Daudet, Alfred de Musset, Victor Hugo, Alexandre Dumas, and George Sand were the leaders of a new and exciting literature. Berlioz, Rossini, Paganini, Liszt, Meyerbeer, and Chopin dominated the musical scene. There were painters, philosophers and scientists on every hand. But nothing pleased Mendelssohn. He scarcely bothered to make contact with the new artistic movement. So far as he was concerned the revolutionaries were too blatant, too deliberately 'romantic', too eager to make every page a page of auto-biography. He gave concerts with great success, but for the rest stood aside. He preferred to appear the cultivated gentleman, rather than adopt the fashionable pose of 'bohemian' artist.

Perhaps this slightly patronizing attitude helped to sour his relations with the orchestra of the Paris Conservatoire. For when they came to re-hearse his new symphony, *The Reformation*, the musicians flatly rejected it as 'too heavy, too many fugatos, too little melody'. It was the kind of criticism he was not accustomed to, and all the more unpalatable for con-taining a large element of truth.

His mood soon turned from irritability to the deepest depression. News came from Germany that his friend Eduard Rietz had died, and then, shortly afterwards, of the death of Goethe. He lingered in Paris only long enough to recover from a mild attack of cholera, then he packed his bags and made tracks for the one country where he felt sure of a welcome: England.

He was received with open arms—not only by friends, but by ordinary musicians, who greeted him with spontaneous applause when he entered the concert-hall unannounced. And despite more grievous news from home (this time of Zelter's death), his mood brightened.

In May, a performance of *The Hebrides* overture delighted everyone. 'Works such as this,' wrote one critic, 'are like angels' visits and should be

Songs Without Words: Book 5, No. 3

made the most of.' Equally successful were performances of the G minor Piano Concerto and a new *Capriccio Brillant* for piano and orchestra, written especially for London.

By the time Mendelssohn had completed arrangements with Novello's publishing house to bring out the first volume of his *Songs Without Words*, he was as completely in love with London as London was with him, and the future seemed rosy.

A holiday sketch by Mendelssohn

57

VIII

Defeat and Success

Despite the fact that Mendelssohn had matured very considerably during his travels, and more than proved his ability to stand on his own feet, the problem of his future career was still a matter for discussion by the family as a whole. Any suggestion that he should allow himself to be supported by the family fortune while he explored and developed his gifts as a composer was unanimously discounted. So far as the Mendelssohns were concerned music was a profession like any other, and it was the professional's duty to support himself and make a success of his career. The idea that creative genius owes its first duty to itself, does not seem to have occurred to any of them.

In accepting his family's set of values, Mendelssohn brought about his own tragedy. He became, it is true, as noble a professional as they could have wished—but only at the expense of his creative gifts. He continued to write splendid music (whenever the crowded timetable of his professional life allowed), and there is no positive sign that his genius ever diminished. But there is strong evidence to suggest that it was never fully explored. It is one of the major tragedies of music that so dazzlingly gifted a mind should have allowed itself to be distracted by petty routines that any one of a hundred ordinary talents could have carried out.

It was decided: Felix had to have an official post—a respectable career. To the family the next step was obvious: he must apply for the post of Director of the Berlin Singakademie. Now that Zelter was dead, who could be a more fitting heir?

Mendelssohn himself was less certain. He would be one of several candidates in what would undoubtedly be a fierce and bitter competition. And he was by no means certain that he wanted to stay in Berlin—after his experiences abroad, it now seemed provincial, narrow-minded and stifling. But family and friends insisted, and so, reluctantly, he allowed his name to go forward.

58

From that moment everything began to go wrong. Malicious tongues gossiped that the Mendelssohns were trying to buy their way to power. It was unthinkable, they said, that an institute founded to sing Christian music should be placed in the hands of a Jew. Mendelssohn was nothing but a spoiled brat, playing at music.

When the votes were counted it was found that Mendelssohn had been soundly defeated. A mood of repentance made itself felt, and he was offered the post of Vice-President as a consolation prize (now that he had been taught a lesson it would be foolish to lose his services altogether, for there was no doubt that he was gifted). Politely, he declined the offer.

Two suggestions now came from outside Berlin and saved him from complete despair. The first was from the Philharmonic Society of London: a request for 'a symphony, an overture, and a vocal piece', handsomely backed by a fee of one hundred guineas (equal to about £1,000 today). The second came from Düsseldorf: an invitation to direct the 1833 Lower Rhine Festival of Music. He accepted both challenges with delight.

Rough sketches for an *Italian* symphony had existed since 1830, awaiting just such an occasion as the London offer. Mendelssohn now polished and brought them to perfection. As a token of gratitude for the 'pleasure and honour' that the Philharmonic Society had 'again conferred on him', he decided to offer them two overtures: a *Trumpet Overture* (written originally in 1825 but now completely revised), and the overture *A Calm Sea and Prosperous Voyage*, based on a poem by Goethe. The 'vocal piece', however, would have to wait until the following year and another visit.

London received him like a native son. The symphony was performed on 13th May with the greatest success. 'It is,' wrote one critic, 'a composition that will endure for ages.' So far as England was concerned, Mendelssohn could do no wrong. A fourth visit was promised for June, to launch the *Trumpet Overture*.

Between the London engagements, however, there was the challenge of Düsseldorf.

The Lower Rhine Festival, which began in 1817, was held each year at Düsseldorf, Cologne, or Aachen. From the moment that Mendelssohn took a hand in its organization (he gave his services on seven occasions, the last being in 1846), the Festival began to assume the greatest importance in German musical life. Great composers thought it an honour to be asked to conduct, and many important works were heard for the first time at its concerts.

Mendelssohn's first Festival Programme included performances of

Handel's oratorio *Israel in Egypt* and Beethoven's *Pastoral* symphony, as well as many minor, now forgotten pieces. Typically, his father put in an appearance, in order to see if Felix could really carry the responsibility of a festival of this size and importance. He received a great surprise. Not only was his son in complete control of his job, but he was the idol of both the general public and his fellow musicians. 'I have never yet seen anyone carried around on a silken cushion as Felix is here,' he wrote.

At the end of the festival Mendelssohn was appointed director of all musical activities for the next three years, at a salary of 600 thalers (about (£1,000). He was also promised three months' vacation a year. In return he was to direct the city's church music, the local choral and orchestral societies, and organize the festivals. Having set himself the task of becoming the busiest professional musician in all Europe, it was a challenge after his own heart.

With the festival safely delivered, Mendelssohn turned again to London. This time, however, he persuaded his father to accompany him—rather as if he wanted to give a final proof of his standing in the musical world. Again, Abraham Mendelssohn was to have reason to look at his son in a new light: the warmth of London's reception was startling.

By the end of September Mendelssohn was fully installed in his first official post. He had every intention of raising the standard of musical life in Düsseldorf. He would be a new broom and sweep clean.

There were the inevitable difficulties. When he began to replace what he regarded as 'frivolous' church music with masses and motets by Palestrina and Lassus, some of the faithful were upset. When he announced a new policy for the opera house, which involved raising the price of seats, there was a minor riot. But, on the whole, things went smoothly and he was soon able to write home and say that he could not wish for 'a more agreeable position'.

It was not long before his mood changed. The opera house got the better of him. He was not accustomed to the intrigues and quarrels that are part and parcel of all theatrical life. Instead of allowing them to wash lightly over him, he took them to heart. Suddenly, and with little thought for his responsibility to the public, he handed the opera house to his assistant conductor and bowed himself out.

Abraham Mendelssohn was furious when he heard the news, and made his feelings very clear. But it was too late for amends: Mendelssohn had harmed his reputation.

By the end of 1834, however, the chance came for a new start. The governing board of the Leipzig Gewandhaus Orchestra, whose concerts dated from the time when Bach himself was cantor at the St. Thomas School, asked him if he would consider becoming their conductor. After insisting that no other musician was to be driven out by his coming, and that he must be allowed five or six months each year for creative work, Mendelssohn agreed on a two-year engagement.

A sketch by Mendelssohn

IX

Leipzig and Marriage

Everything about Leipzig pleased him. After the worry and responsibility of Düsseldorf he felt that he had arrived 'in Paradise'. Although the Gewandhaus Orchestra was rather small (a mere forty players, and nothing in comparison with the monster orchestra he had used to accompany the massed choirs of the 1834 Lower Rhine Festival) it was material that could be worked upon and moulded to his own way of thinking. Leipzig was, moreover, the seat of an ancient and world-famous university—which, to a man of Mendelssohn's culture and intelligence, meant the presence of stimulating minds and an atmosphere of intellectual inquiry. Best of all, Leipzig was that much nearer Berlin. For now that his parents were growing old and no longer enjoyed the best of health (his father was all but blind), it was essential to visit them as often as possible.

After two rehearsals with his new orchestra, Mendelssohn presented himself to the citizens of Leipzig on 4th October 1835 with the following programme:

Overture: *Calm Sea and Prosperous Voyage*	Mendelssohn
Scene and Aria from *Der Freischütz*	Weber
Violin Concerto No. 8	Spohr
Overture and Introduction to *Ali Baba*	Cherubini

INTERVAL

Symphony No. 4	Beethoven

The concert was a great success. It was obvious to everybody that Mendelssohn was the man for the job.

Having made his point, however, he now began a policy of reform. He demanded, and eventually won, an increase in salary for his orchestral players. He then introduced a pension scheme. He began to enlarge the orchestra and improve the pattern of concert programmes. Most important of all: he imposed on them his own ideas of what a conductor should do—ideas that were extremely advanced at the time.

Conducting was something of a novelty in the early part of the nineteenth century. The idea of having someone to beat time had emerged only gradually, but it was still by no means clear whether the time-beater was in charge of the orchestra, or whether the leader of the violins took precedence. The idea that the time-beater should in any way 'interpret' the music was quite novel.

The Music Conservatory, Leipzig

But interpretation was what Mendelssohn believed in. He demanded a precise obedience in matters of phrasing, dynamics, and tone-colour, as well as speed. He was in every sense a perfectionist, and his example set the pace for conductors throughout Europe, creating, as it were, a new branch in the art of music.

And because he took his position as an orchestral conductor seriously, he was also able to use his influence to perform music that had been neglected or misunderstood. In 1839, for example, he gave the first performance of Schubert's great C major Symphony which Schumann had rescued from a pile of dusty manuscripts a few months earlier. He gave performances of

Left: a portrait of Mendelssohn by Steinbrüch; *below:* a portrait by Vernet

Mendelssohn playing for Queen Victoria and Prince Albert,
a painting by Carl Rohling

Beethoven's Ninth Symphony—a rare item in those days; and made his orchestra available even to those composers, such as Berlioz, whose music he did not personally enjoy or understand.

When he was not occupied with the orchestra, Mendelssohn concerned himself mainly with composition. Describing his daily routine in Leipzig, he says that he always rose early and worked at composition until noon. Then he would take a walk and lunch with friends. In the afternoon he would play the piano (he never spoke of 'practising' as such), compose again in the early evening and then eat supper. Sometimes other composers would visit him—Chopin, Schumann, Rossini, Berlioz and Liszt all found their way to Leipzig. He was, in short, king in his natural element.

Beyond the Leipzig circle, however, several tragedies began to unfold. The first of them concerned his family. In November 1835, his father died, suddenly and without pain. The shock was immense. 'My youth,' he wrote later, 'was over with that day.' Now more than ever he felt obliged to live up to what his father had expected of him. He was head of the family, and gravely aware of all that the position implied.

His immediate reaction was to plunge even deeper into the oratorio that he was writing. *St. Paul* had had his father's enthusiastic approval. Now it was to be his memorial.

Although enormously successful in its day, Mendelssohn's first oratorio has never won a universal acceptance. Save for the first section, which deals with Saul's conversion on the road to Damascus, it is not particularly dramatic, and this has told against it. Like his later and more popular oratorio *Elijah*, it is laid out on a grand scale, but fails to achieve the same natural spaciousness and grandeur. The craftsmanship is solid and the music often very beautiful, but the overall effect is simply a trifle dull.

The composition of *St. Paul* and the excitement of rehearsing it for the first performance at the 1836 Lower Rhine Festival, had helped Mendelssohn to forget the death of his father. But as soon as he was able to relax he began to brood on his own situation. Life seemed to be slipping by, and now that the family was breaking up it suddenly came to him that he was lonely. Already his mother had spoken seriously on the subject of marriage. Now he began to consider the matter for himself.

He did not have to wait long for an answer. During a short visit to Frankfurt he met the daughter of an old and highly respected Huguenot family: Cecile Jeanrenaud. He began by flirting with her—as he did with almost every pretty young woman. He ended by falling deeply in love.

At first he kept the news from his mother and eldest sister, and confided

E

in Rebecca—the only really light-hearted member of the family, and the one least likely to see dangers where there were none. As soon as an engagement had been agreed upon, however, he announced his intentions and watched the apprehensions grow.

There was, in fact, nothing to be apprehensive about. Cecile was beautiful and of good family. She was not particularly intelligent or musical, but she was kind-hearted, calm, and sensible. She would bring domestic order and tranquillity into his busy life. She was just the kind of wife his excitable, highly-strung nature was most in need of.

They married in March 1837, but none of Mendelssohn's immediate family circle was present at the ceremony. On the surface, the reasons seem acceptable enough: illness, a detestation of long journeys, old age. But it is also likely that, though they could not find grounds for genuine disapproval, the family felt hurt, unconsulted, shut out by his sudden burst of independent action. The coldness lasted until the birth of his first child, and only then was the relationship resumed with anything like the old warmth and intimacy.

In the meantime, musical life went on. A performance of *St. Paul* had been arranged for the 1837 Birmingham Festival, and Mendelssohn was therefore obliged to prepare for a fifth visit to England. For once in his life he felt reluctant to travel:

> Here I sit—in the fog—very cross—without my wife. It is nine days since I parted from Cecile at Düsseldorf. The first few were quite bearable, though very wearisome, but now that I have got into the whirl of London—great distances—too many people—my head crammed with business and accounts and money matters and arrangements—it is becoming unbearable, and I wish I were sitting with Cecile and had let Birmingham be Birmingham, and could enjoy life more than I do today.

Even so, his visit was a triumphant success, and he returned once more with a torrent of applause ringing in his ears.

Songs Without Words: Book 2, No. 3

X

Berlin

It would have been understandable if Mendelssohn had now chosen to relax. His marriage was a success, and, in due course, he became the father of four children. He was admired and respected throughout the musical world. The demand for his compositions was insatiable: he only had to lift his pen and publishers would fall over themselves competing for the privilege of adding his name to their lists. He was not obliged to work for a living. He need do nothing that did not accord with his tastes.

Yet relaxation was the one thing he avoided. During the last ten years of his life, the dizzying round of work gathered more and more momentum. He conducted, he organized, he taught, he composed, he travelled, and he tried to live a normal social life. Whatever it was that drove him, would not let him rest. Had he deliberately planned to work himself to death, he could scarcely have organized his last years more effectively.

As composer: he completed three String Quartets and a String Quintet, two Piano Trios, two 'Cello Sonatas and a Violin Sonata, six Organ Sonatas, the *Variations Sérieuses* for piano, five books of *Songs Without Words*, and a large handful of miscellaneous piano pieces; the *Scottish* symphony, the Violin Concerto in E minor, the symphony-cantata *Hymn of Praise*; the oratorio *Elijah* and the overture *Ruy Blas*; some twenty settings of religious words—for chorus and orchestra, chorus and organ, or chorus alone; thirty songs, forty partsongs, and a number of vocal duets; and the incidental music to four major theatrical productions. He left unfinished at his death: the opera *Loreley* and the oratorio *Christus*.

As conductor: he was responsible for the Gewandhaus Orchestra, the Berlin Cathedral Choir, and the subscription concerts in Berlin. He directed three German music festivals, and two English music festivals, and gave concert-series in England on five occasions.

As teacher and administrator: he founded the Leipzig Conservatory and took an active part as professor of piano and composition; and he wasted

Variations Sérieuses: Theme and first variation

much time and energy in trying to create a similar institution in Berlin.
And all the time his health deteriorated.

Mendelssohn's obsession with work may in part be attributed to his up-bringing—wealth and success made all the Mendelssohn family nervous of appearing idle and frivolous. But it also suggests a certain basic, inner uncertainty—as if to relax, even for a moment, would be to admit defeat. And it is evident from the whole pattern of his last years that he was a deeply disturbed, unhappy man. What it was that threw him off balance can only be guessed at: but it is at least arguable that, unconsciously, he was wrestling with the dreadful foreboding of an early death.

Perhaps this is also why some of his later works are weighed down by what can only be described as 'moral earnestness'. They seem designed to be 'great', but only succeed in being ponderous. It is as if he felt obliged to discredit the carefree days of youth, when he might dream his 'Midsummer Night's Dream' and make musical sketches of his holidays in the Hebrides, and erect in their place some monument of irreproachable respectability and conventional piety.

Fortunately Mendelssohn was not always able to restrain that sense of humorous delight and poetic fantasy that were the true sources of his great-ness. And if any single proof were needed that his creative gifts did not desert him during these final years, it could be found in the flawless Violin Concerto of 1844. Without in any way striving after effect, it achieves the same kind of easy perfection that is the hallmark of his finest youthful works.

The pattern of Mendelssohn's last years is governed by his duties as con-

From the *Festgesang*

Allegro moderato
UNISON

Here with — in our coun-try's bor-ders First the gold — en day began. Ger-man peo — ple, it was you who Saw the dawn of mod — ern
man.__ Gu — ten – berg,__ the Ger — man son,__
__ Gu — ten – berg, the Ger — man son, Lit the__ torch for ev' – ry –

-one, Gu — ten – berg, the Ger — man son, Lit the__ torch for ev' – ry – one.

etc.

ductor and administrator. He remained faithful to Leipzig until 1841, taking time off for composition and occasional trips abroad as the terms of his contract allowed. The compositions of this period include an overture to Victor Hugo's play *Ruy Blas* (still a great favourite with orchestras), and two works written in 1840 for the Leipzig ceremonies to commemorate the invention of printing by Johann Gutenburg: the *Hymn of Praise* and the *Festgesang* (Festival Song).

Though popular in its day, the *Hymn of Praise* is now seldom performed, except by amateurs. It has met this fate partly because the level of Mendelssohn's inspiration sometimes flags, and partly because the form of the work is unsatisfactory. With equal justification it can be regarded as a four-movement symphony with a lengthy choral finale, or as a cantata with an elaborate three-movement orchestral introduction: there is nothing in the sweep and line of the music to suggest its true nature. And, of course, it prompts comparison with Beethoven's Ninth Symphony!

The *Festgesang*, on the other hand, has won for itself an unexpected immortality. Designed to be sung in the open air, on the single occasion of the unveiling of a statue to Gutenberg, it would have been forgotten had it not contained one very splendid tune. This was rescued and is now sung all over the world to the words: 'Hark! the Herald Angels Sing.'

So long as he was concerned only with Leipzig's musical affairs, Mendelssohn's life, though busy, was reasonably calm and ordered. In 1841, however, the new king of Prussia, Frederick William IV, decided to found an Academy of Arts in Berlin and offered him the post of Director. Tempted by the honour, the handsome salary, and the fact that he could return to Berlin and take an active part in the family once more, Mendelssohn accepted. He now had two administrative jobs: at Leipzig *and* Berlin.

Had Frederick William's proposals been backed by deeds, all might still have been well. But beyond the grandiose desire to have an Academy of Arts, everything else was vague. The directorship, and for a time the handsome salary, existed only on paper. Mendelssohn tried to get things moving, but met with nothing but frustration. Precious hours that should have been given to music vanished in the battle against official incompetence. He grew tired and irritable, and was at last reduced to complete despair. By the end of the year he had to admit defeat. He returned to Leipzig, promising, however, to place himself at the king's disposal for another year as soon as the position of the Academy had been clarified.

The only positive result of his Berlin venture was the composition of incidental music to a series of plays—carried out, as it were, by royal command. *Antigone* (1841), *Athalie* (1845), and *Oedipus at Colonnus* (1845) all received his meticulous attention; but the production of *A Midsummer Night's Dream* (1842) touched his heart, and brought about a miraculous renewal of the spirit of the music he had written when he was seventeen.

Violin Concerto in E minor: second movement

But these were small gains compared with the waste of time and energy spent in trying to realize the king's dream. For three years, Frederick William continued to play upon Mendelssohn's suicidal sense of duty, and it was only in 1844 that he allowed him to abandon the project as hopeless.

Mendelssohn's chorus for *Antigone*, a cartoon from *Punch*

During these nerve-racking years there were, nevertheless, certain triumphs and delights. He directed successful festivals at Düsseldorf, and Dresden in 1842, and at Zweibrücken in the following year. In the summer of 1842 he also made his seventh journey to England, performing the *Scottish* symphony (completed at last) with great success at a Philharmonic Society concert. It was during this visit that he met the young Queen Victoria and her husband.

Mendelssohn's reception at Buckingham Palace was typical of the ease and friendliness he met in all his relations with England. He talked first with Prince Albert, who was himself an accomplished musical amateur. Soon they began to examine old volumes of music, spreading them over the tables and chairs. When the Queen came in, she began to tidy up their muddle like any conscientious housewife. Then Prince Albert played a chorale on the small chamber organ, and Mendelssohn followed him with improvisations on themes from *St. Paul*. Not to be outdone, the Queen declared she would sing some of Mendelssohn's songs, and, after a frantic hunt for the music, duly did so—'neatly, in strict time, and with very nice interpretation', thought Mendelssohn. When the Queen discovered that the song had really been composed by Fanny (Mendelssohn published several of his sister's pieces: it would have been improper for a young lady of her social position to appear before the public as a composer), she was delighted. And so the visit continued: charming, unaffected, spontaneous —a far cry from court life in Berlin.

XI

The End

By November 1844, Mendelssohn had obtained his release both from Leipzig and Berlin. He left Leipzig with a sense of duty well done. The Conservatory of Music, which he had established in the previous year, showed every sign of flourishing; and the citizens of Leipzig were more than satisfied with his work. Berlin he left with nothing but a sense of relief.

He now made his home in Frankfurt, determined to retire from public life. For a while he stood by his decision. He refused a tempting offer from New York, and even one from his beloved England. He immersed himself in composition: a String Quintet, a Piano Trio, and, most important of all, the oratorio *Elijah*.

By the middle of 1845, however, his Leipzig friends had argued him into returning to direct concerts and teaching at the Conservatory; and from that moment the frantic cycle of work began to build up again.

In May and June 1846 Mendelssohn directed his last Lower Rhine Festival and then left immediately for London, to begin preliminary rehearsals for the first performance of *Elijah*, which was to be given at the Birmingham Festival on 26th August.

The success of that first performance was overwhelming. *The Times*, in reporting it, leaves no room for doubt:

> The last note of *Elijah* was drowned in a long-continued unanimous volley of plaudits, vociferous and deafening. It was as though enthusiasm, long checked, had suddenly burst its bounds and filled the air with shouts of exultation. Mendelssohn, evidently overpowered, bowed his acknowledgement and quickly descended from his position in the conductor's rostrum; but he was compelled to appear again, amidst renewed cheers and huzzas. Never was there a more complete triumph—never a more thorough and speedy recognition of a great work of art.

76

Leipzig 8th Febr. 1847

My Dear Sir

I send you with these lines the last Chorus of Elijah. Now I have only the song which is to come in at the beginning of no 8, and as soon as that will be finished I will not tease you any more about alterations and all that, for you have now the whole work in hands. But pray do not forget to postpone the engraving of no. 8 until I send you that song! All the rest may be forthwith engraved.

While I wrote the alterations in the Chorus no. 40 (in my last letter) I forgot to write that there is also one in the Accompaniment of that passage. So please to correct bars 47, 48, and 49 (they are the last but two of the last page but one of that Chorus) thus:

As for the story of the Opera my friend Klingemann will tell you all about it, as I have written it at length to him; and I am so over loaded with Leipsic music, & with letters & with all sorts of things that you must excuse me if I refer you to him & cannot repeat again what I wrote about that story.

Always very truly yours

Leipsic 8th Febr. 1847.

Felix Mendelssohn Bartholdy.

P.S. I am now almost sure that I shall be able to leave here on the

A letter from Mendelssohn concerning the publication of *Elijah*

The End

It was the outstanding moment of his enormously successful career, and *Elijah* seemed the crown of his life's work.

He returned home with plans for revising the oratorio, beginning a new one (*Christus*), and writing an opera. He also had plans for relaxing—when he could find time.

Elijah: 'Lord God of Abraham'

*The part of Elijah is sung by a baritone, and therefore sounds an octave lower.

'Lord God of Abraham' in Mendelssohn's own handwriting

The End

But he never allowed himself the chance. He agreed to return to England in April 1847 for more performances of *Elijah*, in London, Manchester, and Birmingham. He would conduct performances of the *Scottish* symphony and the *Midsummer Night's Dream* music. He would appear as soloist in Beethoven's G major Piano Concerto, and support the London début of his friend Jenny Lind. He would go to receptions and wait upon the Queen at Buckingham Palace. He would even find time to visit his friends.

But it was obvious that something was wrong. His friends noticed that 'he had aged, looked pale and weary, walked less quickly than before, and was more intensely affected by any passing thing than he used to be'. It would need very little to throw him completely off balance.

What came was a disaster of the greatest magnitude. He completed his English engagements and had scarcely been two days with his wife and family, when news came that his beloved sister had died from a sudden paralytic stroke. His father's death had been a severe blow; his mother's, in 1842 also. But this shattered everything. With a cry, he fell to the floor insensible.

He lived for less than six months. Outwardly he gave himself to music (the powerful F minor String Quartet belongs to this period), but inwardly he grieved and was fearful. On 9th September his health began to fail. He rallied, but it failed again. On 7th November a stroke rendered him unconscious and on the following day he died. He was thirty-eight years old.

Two sketches drawn by Mendelssohn during his honeymoon; *above*: 'lunch at Strasberg';
below: 'a charming display at the milliner's'

Portraits of Mendelssohn and his wife, Cecile, by Eduard Magnus

XII

Aftermath

At the time of his death, Mendelssohn's reputation seemed assured. To most European music-lovers he was, quite simply, one of the great masters. Had anyone suggested that within a hundred years the citizens of Leipzig would tear down the statue their forefathers had erected to his honour, and that in England critics would arise to pour scorn on his music, he would have been laughed out of court. In 1847 Mendelssohn stood for everything that was noblest and best in European music, everything that was most likely to endure.

Reaction began in Germany itself shortly after his death. Fanned by Wagner's fanatical anti-Semitic writings it soon outstripped purely musical misgivings, to become a personal vendetta which reached its climax in 1937 with the Nazi decision to strike Mendelssohn's name from the roll of German culture.

In less troubled parts of Europe it was not Mendelssohn's religion that told against him, but an inevitable change of taste that led certain critics to see in his music all that they most disliked of the nineteenth century.

Caught between these tendencies, Mendelssohn's reputation sank like lead, and it was to be many years before a more realistic appreciation of his actual worth could even be attempted.

Although a balance has now been struck between the wild adoration that greeted Mendelssohn in his lifetime and the equally wild vilification of those who reacted against it, he remains a problematic figure. Is he to be regarded as a second-rate major composer, or a first-rate minor master? Should he be classed as a romantic with strong classical tendencies, or as a classicist who happened also to have a romantic streak? Did he ever really develop beyond the youthful brilliance of the Octet? In his anxiety to be liked by everyone, did he perhaps tame his imagination to the point where it became dull and all too predictable?

The truth of the matter may well lie in this very ambiguity. Mendelssohn

F

was all of these things—a contradiction even to himself. Able to charm at the surface level, as so many of the delightful *Songs Without Words* prove, he could also rise, with Bach-like intensity, to the heights of the fugal overture and opening chorus of *Elijah*. Within the strictest confines of classical form he could accommodate the richest vein of delicate poetic fancy, to produce a *Midsummer Night's Dream* or *The Hebrides* overture—both masterpieces of the highest order. The empty glitter of the *Capriccio brillant* can be matched by the power and depth of the *Variations Sérieuses*. The Violin Concerto in E minor, though bludgeoned by countless hacks, still remains one of the great concertos. And if perhaps the *Reformation* symphony now seems a trifle heavy-handed, its shortcomings are more than offset by the charm and vivacity of the *Scottish* and *Italian* symphonies.

Even in the treacherous field of chamber music Mendelssohn was at ease: the three string quartets of Opus 44 are both fluent and highly imaginative, and at least one of them (the Quartet in E flat major) measures up to the supreme standard set by Beethoven. The Octet is in a class by itself.

Although it would be foolish to deny that his music has its limitations, Mendelssohn remains one of the few nineteenth-century composers in whose work ends and means are perfectly matched. His craftsmanship was at all times superb—the perfect foil to his delicate imagination. Unlike some of his contemporaries, he was not interested in expressing passion in the grand romantic manner. But this does not mean that his music is cold and unfeeling. The emotion is there, but does not call attention to itself, or do anything that he would have considered uncivilized or ill-mannered. For the music is like the man: intelligent and imaginative, tender and poetic, lively and graceful—in every way an agreeable companion.

Suggestions for Further Reading

Curiously, there are few reliable modern accounts of Mendelssohn's life and works. Nineteenth-century studies abound—but are mostly spoiled by a concern to create legends of almost supernatural virtue and unqualified achievement. For the same reason, the early translations of his letters are sadly in need of revision, which would include the restoration of those passages that suggest the composer's human failings. Of these early accounts, only that by Sir George Grove, as it appeared in the *first* edition of *Grove's Dictionary*, is still worth seeking out. It was reprinted in 1951 in book form, under the title: *Beethoven; Schubert; Mendelssohn.*

The following modern accounts can be recommended:

Mendelssohn, by Eric Werner (Macmillan, 1963)
Mendelssohn, by Philip Radcliffe (Dent, *Master Musicians*, 1954)
Mendelssohn Letters, a selection by G. Selden-Goth (Elek, 1946)

Summary of Mendelssohn's Works

Choral Works with Orchestra

St. Paul (oratorio), 1836
Hymn of Praise (symphony-cantata), 1840
The First Walpurgis Night (cantata), 1832; revised 1843
Elijah (oratorio), 1846
Lauda Sion (cantata), 1846

Orchestral Works

Symphony No. 1, in C minor, 1842
Symphony No. 3, in A (*Scottish*), 1842
Symphony No. 4, in A (*Italian*), 1843
Symphony No. 5, in D major (*Reformation*), 1832
Overture: *A Midsummer Night's Dream*, 1826
Overture: *The Hebrides*, 1832
Overture: *Calm Sea and Prosperous Voyage*, 1832
Overture: *The Fair Melusine*, 1833
Overture: *Ruy Blas*, 1839
Overture in C major (*Trumpet*), 1829

Concertos

Piano Concerto No. 1, in G minor, 1831
Piano Concerto No. 2, in D minor, 1837
Violin Concerto, in E minor, 1844

Summary of Mendelssohn's Works

Chamber Music

Six String Quartets; two String Quintets; two Piano Trios; one Piano Sextet; one Octet for Strings

Piano music includes eight books of *Songs Without Words,* and there are many songs and vocal pieces.

Index

86

Index